A New True Book

SQUIRRELS

By Emilie U. Lepthien

CHILDRENS PRESS®
CHICAGO

Tuft-eared squirrel

Project Editor: Fran Dyra
Design: Margrit Fiddle

PHOTO CREDITS

© Reinhard Brucker—2, 35 (left)

H. Armstrong Roberts—25 (right); © E.R.
Degginger, 5 (bottom right), 31 (right)

© Jerry Hennen—13, 21, 29

Historical Pictures—40 (bottom), 43

© Emilie Lepthien—27

North Wind Picture Archives—40 (top)

Photri—4 (right), 7 (left); © Leonard Lee Rue III,
19; © Rob & Melissa Simpson, 33 (left);
© Biedel, 44 (left); © Lani, 44 (right)

Root Resources—© Alan G. Nelson, Cover;
© Anthony Blueman, 36 (right)

Tom Stack & Associates—© Thomas Kitchin,
15; © Cris Crowley, 35 (center right); © Richard
P. Smith, 42 (left); © Mary Clay, 42 (right)

© Lynn M. Stone—30

TSW-CLICK/Chicago—© Leonard Lee Rue III, 5
(left), 31 (left); © Gary Bumgarner, 17, 18

Valan—© Wayne Lankinen, 4 (left), 8, 28, 33
(right), 34, 45; © Albert Kuhnigk, 5 (top right),
35 (top right & bottom right); © Jeff Foott, 7
(right), 11; © Stephen J Krasemann, 10;
© Michel Bourque, 9; © J.R. Page, 22; © Harold
V. Green, 12, 39; © Kennon Cooke, 25 (left);
© John Cancalosi, 36 (left); © Dennis W.
Schmidt, 37

Cover—Fox squirrel

Library of Congress Cataloging-in-Publication Data

Lepthien, Emilie U. (Emilie Utteg)
    Squirrels / by Emilie U. Lepthien.
        p.   cm. — (A New true book)
    Includes index.
    Summary: Discusses the varieties, physical
characteristics, behavior, and life cycle of squirrels.
    ISBN 0-516-01947-3
    1. Squirrels—Juvenile literature. [1. Squirrels.]
I. Title.
QL737.R68L45   1992
599.32'32—dc20   92-9207
                                            CIP
                                            AC

TABLE OF CONTENTS

Squirrels Around the World...4

Tree Squirrels...7

Summer and Winter Coats...10

Coat Colors...14

Squirrel Bodies...16

Special Teeth and Jaws...21

Noses and Whiskers...24

Grooming...26

Leafy Homes...27

Baby Squirrels...31

Flying Squirrels...33

Ground Squirrels...35

Squirrels and People...41

Words You Should Know...46

Index...47

The red squirrel (left) and the gray squirrel (right) are the most common squirrels in North America.

SQUIRRELS AROUND THE WORLD

There are over 300 kinds of squirrels, and they live in many countries of the world. Squirrels are rodents—animals that have long, sharp front teeth.

California ground squirrel
(above), Arctic ground squirrel
(top right), and southern
flying squirrel (right)

There are three large
groups of squirrels. Two
groups, the tree squirrels
and the ground squirrels,
are active during the day.
Flying, or gliding, squirrels

are active at dusk and during the night.

Some squirrels live in deserts. Others live on the tundra of the far north, on prairies, or in forests. Gray and fox squirrels have adapted to life in towns and cities, on farms, and wherever people live.

Squirrels are hunted for food by coyotes, foxes, mountain lions, and other predators.

Gray squirrel (above)
Fox squirrel (right)

TREE SQUIRRELS

Gray squirrels and fox squirrels are the most common tree squirrels in North America. Both kinds live in the eastern half of the United States and part of Canada.

7

Red squirrels
are able to eat
some mushrooms
that are harmful
to people.

Gray squirrels like
forests. Fox squirrels like
more open land and the
edges of forests.

Red squirrels, or pine
squirrels, live in evergreen
forests. They are found in

Alaska, northern Canada, the northern Middle West, and the northwestern states.

Tree squirrels are active throughout the year.

Squirrels are very alert and active. They chatter to each other as they scamper about.

SUMMER AND WINTER COATS

In summer, squirrels have short, soft, lightweight fur coats. Their tails are thin.

In winter, squirrels grow a thick, soft undercoat to

Some people think that squirrels can predict the weather. If their tails are thick and bushy, the winter will be cold.

Squirrels grow warm winter coats. In colder areas, some fur grows on their feet.

keep them warm. Long guard hairs cover the undercoat. The guard hairs shed water and snow.

In northern climates, some fur grows on their feet in winter. The fur keeps their feet warm. It

11

also helps them grip slippery branches.

Squirrels use their tails as blankets to keep their nose and face warm in winter when they sleep. When squirrels rest outside, they fold the tail over their back to save body heat.

Squirrels in northern

A red squirrel sits with its tail folded over its back.

Pine squirrel molting in spring. The spring molt takes about six weeks.

climates molt, or shed
their coat, twice a year,
in spring and fall.

The autumn molt starts
in October. By the time
the weather is cold, squirrels
have warm winter coats.

Squirrels that live in
warm climates molt only
once a year.

COAT COLORS

Coat color depends on where tree squirrels live. The color of gray squirrels matches the gray bark on the trees where they live.

Red squirrels have reddish or brown fur to match the bark of pine, spruce, and cedar trees. Some red squirrels have ashy gray sides that blend with the trees that lose their leaves in autumn.

Many squirrels have pale fur on their underside. This

makes them harder to see from below.

Some gray and fox squirrels have dark or black fur.

Some gray squirrels have black fur.

SQUIRREL BODIES

Squirrels have very sharp eyesight. They can see even in dim light. Their dark eyes are set at the sides of their head. They can see all around without moving their head. They can see for greater distances than most rodents.

Squirrels have large ears that can pick up the smallest sound.

Squirrels' front feet are almost like hands. They use them to hold nuts while they crack the shells.

Squirrels' hind feet are large and strong. There are five toes on each hind foot. The front feet have four toes, plus a very small toe like a thumb.

Every toe has a sharp,

17

curved claw.
These claws
hook into
tree bark.
Squirrels
always come
down trees
headfirst.
They hold their
head up so
they can look
for danger.

Squirrel coming down a tree headfirst

A baby gray squirrel climbing a tree. Sometimes squirrels circle around the tree as they climb.

Squirrels climb up trees headfirst, too. They move their hind feet and fore-feet alternately in pairs.

Their hind legs are powerful. Squirrels can leap easily from one branch to another.

19

Squirrels sit on their hind legs when they rest. They use their tail for balance.

The tail is used as a rudder when squirrels swim. It also can be used as an umbrella for shade. Sometimes squirrels use their tail to give danger signals to other squirrels.

Squirrels can crack the hardest nuts with their powerful teeth. They leave a pile of nutshells at their feet.

SPECIAL TEETH AND JAWS

Squirrels have a pair of gnawing teeth, called incisors, in both the upper and lower jaws. The incisors wear down from gnawing. But they continue to grow throughout the

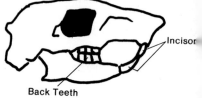

Incisor

Back Teeth

animal's life. Squirrels can crack nuts with their powerful incisors. They hold a nut in their front paws, cut into the shell, and eat the nut inside.

There is a space between the incisors and the molars, or grinding teeth, in the back of the jaw. Each jaw has four pairs of molars.

Squirrels have special jaws. The lower jaw moves forward so that the upper and lower incisors meet when the squirrel is gnawing. The lower jaw also moves slightly back so that the molars can meet when the squirrel is grinding food. Food is ground up with a circular movement of the lower jaw.

NOSES AND WHISKERS

Tree squirrels hide nuts to eat in winter. They dig holes an inch deep, drop in the nuts, and cover them with earth.

Many people think squirrels remember where they hide their nuts. But a squirrel's memory lasts no longer than twenty minutes. Instead, they use their keen sense of smell

No one knows how many trees grow from nuts that squirrels bury in the ground. Whiskers (right) help squirrels to tell if an opening is big enough for them to pass through.

to find food, even under the snow.

Their whiskers are very important, too. Long nose whiskers and whiskers under the head tell the animals if a tree hole is wide enough for them.

GROOMING

Squirrels spend a lot of time grooming themselves. First they moisten their front paws with their tongue and wash their face and neck.

They lick their body fur and hind legs to clean them. They hold their tail between their paws and comb it with their teeth. Then they wash it with their tongue.

LEAFY HOMES

Since tree squirrels do not hibernate, or sleep through the winter, they need shelter throughout the year. Some squirrels build summer homes of leaves and twigs in a tree.

Squirrel's nest high in a tree

Baby squirrels
in their nest

In winter, they find warmer homes in a tree den or hollow.

Some gray squirrels build a nest where a branch forks out from a tree trunk. The nest is lined with dried grass, leaves, shredded bark,

Gray squirrel nest on a tree branch

and twigs. They build a
cover over the nest so it
is comfortable all year.
   Sometimes several
squirrels share a nest.
During stormy weather, they
stay in the nest or den for
several days. But even on
cold, snowy days they climb

A gray squirrel digs for nuts buried under the snow.

down to hunt for food.

Tree squirrels mark their territory in several ways. Sometimes they wipe saliva from their mouth against a branch. The scent marks their territory. They also mark branches with urine. The scent remains even when it rains.

These baby red squirrels (left) are about one month old. Baby gray squirrels (above) explore the world outside their nest.

BABY SQUIRRELS

Gray squirrels and fox squirrels have two litters each year. Three to five babies are born about forty days after their parents mate. The babies weigh only half an ounce

31

at birth. They have no fur,
and their eyes are closed.

Mother squirrels take
good care of their young.
Like other mammals, they
feed their young with their
warm milk.

When the young
squirrels are five or six
weeks old, their eyes are
open and they have all
their fur. They soon learn
to climb out of the nest
and look for their own food.

Flying squirrels are bigger than other squirrels. Their huge eyes help them to see better at night, when they are active.

FLYING SQUIRRELS

Northern flying squirrels are found across southern Canada and the northern United States. Southern flying squirrels live in the eastern half of the United States. They are active at dusk and at night.

A flying squirrel glides through the air.

Flying squirrels do not really fly. They have wide flaps of skin along their sides. When they leap, they spread their legs and glide. The tail acts as a rudder. When they land, they scramble to safety on the far side of a tree.

GROUND SQUIRRELS

There are over forty kinds of ground squirrels. Chipmunks, thirteen-lined ground squirrels, prairie dogs, woodchucks, and

Woodchuck

Prairie dog

Thirteen-lined ground squirrel

Chipmunk

All these animals
are ground squirrels.

Left: Yellow-bellied marmot   Right: A thirteen-lined
ground squirrel carrying grass to its burrow

marmots are all ground
squirrels. Many kinds can
be found in the central
and western states. Since
ground squirrels live in
burrows, they can survive
in almost any climate.
Some hibernate in the

winter. Other kinds estivate, or sleep, during hot summer months.

About four weeks after their parents mate, ground squirrel babies are born. The female makes a nest in an old burrow. She will have from two to eight

A prairie dog mother and her babies stand outside the burrow.

babies to feed and care
for. Her mate leaves her
after mating.

The babies' eyes do not
open for three or four
weeks. They feed on their
mother's milk. Burrows or
dens have several tunnels.
Soon the babies explore
the tunnels. They are
curious about the outside
world. But if they see
danger, they scamper
back into the burrow.

Like tree squirrels,
ground squirrels are awake

A chipmunk
carries a nut
in one of its
cheek pouches.

during the day. They molt
only once a year. In
September they are busy
gathering and storing food.
Some can carry nuts in their
cheek pouches. They hide
the nuts in their burrow.

This drawing from the 1300s (above) shows a man catching squirrels. The Native Americans and European settlers (left) hunted squirrels for food and furs.

SQUIRRELS AND PEOPLE

Native Americans in eastern North America hunted squirrels with bows and arrows and traps. Squirrels provided food and soft fur pelts.

The early European settlers hunted squirrels with their rifles. Pioneer families frequently ate squirrel pie, squirrel stew, or squirrel with dumplings.

Squirrels like to eat farmers' crops, such as corn (right) and apples.

Squirrels found farms inviting. They ate the crops. So the settlers held squirrel-hunting expeditions. Millions of squirrels were killed.

Squirrels also lost their

homes when forests were

Settlers hunting
squirrels with
rifles

cut down. By the year
1900, gray and fox
squirrels were threatened
with extinction. Then many
states limited squirrel
hunting. Now these small

43

mammals have increased
in numbers after learning
to adapt to changes in
their habitat.

Some squirrels in cities
and towns will come right
up to people. But remember,

Squirrels have adapted to life in towns and cities.

squirrels are wild animals.
Sometimes they bite. So
enjoy watching them
from a distance.

WORDS YOU SHOULD KNOW

active (AK • tihv) — awake and moving around

adapt (uh • DAPT) — to change to fit new conditions, such as a
    different climate

alternately (ALL • ter • nit • lee) — first one, and then the other

burrow (BER • oh) — a hole under the ground that an animal uses
    for a home

circular (SER • kyoo • ler) — moving around and around

coyote (kye • OH • tee) — an animal that looks like a small wolf

desert (DEH • zert) — an area of land that gets little rainfall and has
    very dry soil

estivate (ESS • tih • vait) — to sleep, or hibernate, during the
    summer

evergreen (EH • ver • green) — green all year round; trees having
    small green leaves called needles

extinction (ex • TINK • shun) — the dying out of a kind of plant or
    animal

glide (GLYDE) — to float slowly down to the earth

grooming (GROO • ming) — cleaning and combing the fur

habitat (HAB • ih • tat) — the place where a plant or an animal is
    usually found

hibernate (HY • ber • nait) — to go into a state of deep sleep in
    which body temperature drops and breathing slows

incisors (IN • sye • zerz) — long, sharp front teeth

litter (LIT • er) — a group of baby animals born at the same time
    from the same mother

mammal (MAM • il) — one of a group of warm-blooded animals that
    have hair and nurse their young with milk

molars (MOH • lerz) — broad, flat back teeth

molt (MOHLT) — to shed; to lose fur or feathers

pelt (PEHLT) — the skin of an animal; fur

prairie (PRAIR • ee) — land that has few trees and that is covered with grass

predator (PREH • di • ter) — an animal that kills and eats other animals

rodent (RO • dint) — an animal that has long, sharp front teeth for gnawing

saliva (suh • LYE • va) — the watery liquid produced in the mouth

tundra (TUN • dra) — cold lands in the far north, where no trees grow

tunnel (TUN • il) — a hole that makes a path down through the ground

INDEX

Alaska, 9
baby squirrels, 31-32, 37-38
burrows, 36, 38, 39
Canada, 7, 9
chipmunks, 35
claws, 18
climbing, 18-19
colors of squirrels, 14-15
deserts, 6
ears, 16
estivating, 37
European settlers, 41
eyes, 16, 32, 38
farms, 6, 42
feet, 17-18, 19
flying squirrels, 5-6, 33-34
forests, 6, 8, 42
fox squirrels, 6, 7, 8, 15, 31

fur, 10-12, 13, 14, 15, 32, 41
gliding, 34
gray squirrels, 6, 7, 8, 14, 15, 28, 31
grooming, 26
ground squirrels, 5, 35-39
hibernating, 27, 36-37
homes, 27-29
hunting of squirrels, 41, 42, 43
incisors, 21-22, 23
jaws, 21, 23
kinds of squirrels, 4, 5, 35
legs, 19, 20
marking territory, 30
marmots, 36
milk, 32, 38
molars, 22-23

molting, 13, 39
Native Americans, 41
nests, 28-29
nuts, 22, 24, 39
people and squirrels, 6, 41-44
prairie dogs, 35
predators, 6
red squirrels (pine squirrels), 8,
    14
rodents, 4
saliva, 30

tail, 10, 12, 20, 26, 34
teeth, 4, 21-23, 26
thirteen-lined ground squirrels,
    35
towns and cities, 6, 44
tree squirrels, 5, 7-32, 38
trees, 14, 18, 19, 27, 28
tundra, 6
urine, 30
whiskers, 25
woodchucks, 35

About the Author

Emilie U. Lepthien received her BA and MS degrees and certificate in school administration from Northwestern University. She taught upper-grade science and social studies, wrote and narrated science programs for the Chicago Public Schools' station WBEZ, and was principal in Chicago, Illinois, for twenty years. She received the American Educator's Medal from Freedoms Foundation.

She is a member of Delta Kappa Gamma Society International, Chicago Principals' Association, Illinois Women's Press Association, National Federation of Press Women, and AAUW.

She has written books in the Enchantment of the World, New True Books, and America the Beautiful series.